513.2   Smoothey, Marion.
SMO
         Estimating.

$25.64   3800300013063R
                  12/09/1999

DATE			

LET'S INVESTIGATE
Estimating

LET'S INVESTIGATE
Estimating

By Marion Smoothey
Illustrated by Ann Baum

MARSHALL CAVENDISH

NEW YORK • LONDON • TORONTO • SYDNEY

© Marshall Cavendish Corporation 1995

Published by Marshall Cavendish Corporation
2415 Jerusalem Avenue
PO Box 587
North Bellmore
New York 11710

Series created by Graham Beehag Books

Editorial consultant: Prof. Sonia Helton
University of South Florida, St. Petersburg

Library of Congress Cataloging-in-Publication Data

Smoothey, Marion,
      Estimating / by Marion Smoothey : illustrated by Ann Baum.
         p. cm. – (Lets Investigate)
      Includes index.
      ISBN 1-85435-779-4 ISBN 1-854535-773-5 (set)
      1. Mensuration – Juvenile literature. 2. Approximation theory –
Juvenile literature. [1. Approximation theory.] I. Baum, Ann.
ill. II. Title. III. Series: Smoothey, Marion, 1943-   Lets Investigate.
      QA485.S633 1994   94-19142
      513.2'4 – dc20   CIP
                                        AC

Printed in Malaysia by Times Offset (M) SDN BHD

Contents

Introduction

How good are you at judging distance? How long does it take you to walk a mile? How wide is the eye of a needle? Can you tell quickly if you have enough money to buy six items at different prices? Do you know when a pitcher is big enough to hold a carton of milk?

The questions, games, and activities in this book will help you to improve your estimating skills.

You will need a calculator, a measuring tape, a ruler, two dice, and a large measuring cup.

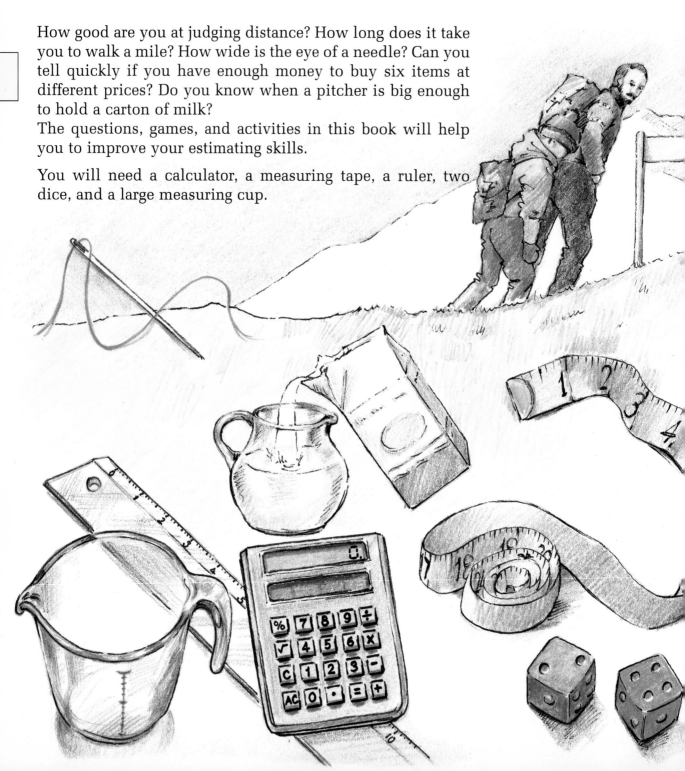

Recognizing Estimates

7

EIGHT THOUSAND SEE THE PANTHERS SHAME

When you see a headline like the one shown left, you might wonder how the reporter knows that there were exactly eight thousand spectators at the game. The answer is that she probably doesn't and there probably weren't. It is more likely that she is making an estimate of the numbers of people in the crowd.

An estimate is an intelligent guess. It is not a number picked at random but one based on observation and reasoning. Nor is it a lie or a mistake. Sometimes all you need is a good estimate, not an exact answer.

Another word for an estimate is an approximation. When you see words like ``about,'' ``approximately,'' ``over,'' ``under,'' and "nearly," they are clues that an estimate is being used.

● Which of these statements are estimates?

1. More than 15% buy cheese once a week.

2. Approximately one child in three under the age of 7 cannot read.

3. Tom has about a million hairs on his head.

8

4. 18½ million people use trains in Japan everyday.

5. In 1964 an earthquake in Prince William Sound, Alaska, measured 8.5 on the Richter Scale. It lasted 7 minutes.

6. Five candy bars at 50 cents each cost $2.50.

7. The Appalachians are 250 million years old.

8. If 40 children travel on a 37-seat bus, 3 will not have a seat.

9. Helena works for 6 hours at $5 per hour; she earns $30.

10. Sydney, Australia is 14 times further away from London than Venice is.

About How Many?

The reporter at the Panther's game could use several methods to estimate the number of people there.

She could ask the management how many people went through the turnstiles or how many tickets they sold. These estimates would be very close to the actual number of people at the game.

● **1.** Why are these numbers probably not exactly the same as the number of people at the game?

She could find out the total capacity of the stadium, estimate what fraction of it was empty, and figure out an estimate from that.

● **2.** How can you make an estimate of how many people this stadium will hold?

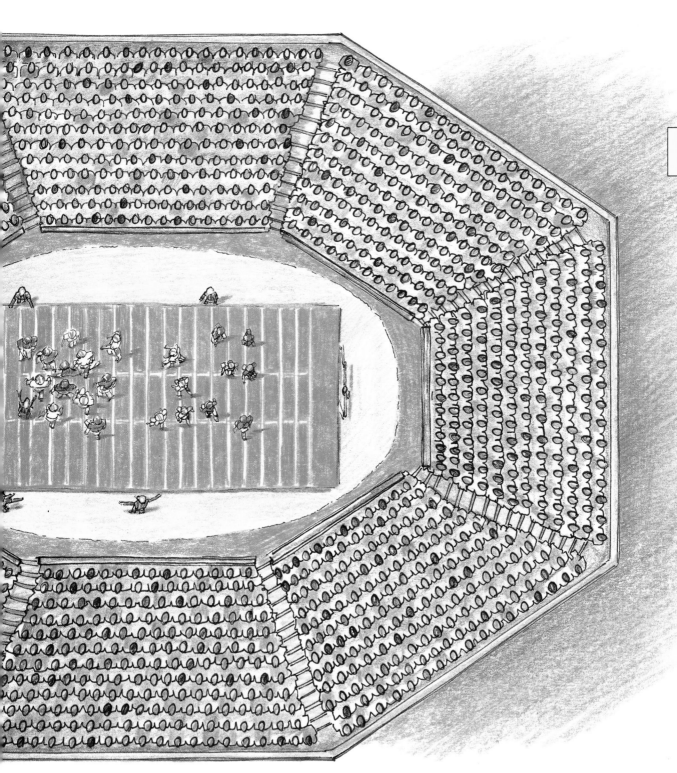

One way to solve a problem that involves large numbers is to think about a similar problem with small numbers.

How many candies do you estimate are on this dish?

12

Just make an estimate; you do not need to count the candies one by one. You can see that the candies are arranged in three approximately equal groups. There are about seven in each group. Three groups of about seven means there are about twenty one candies all together ($3 \times 7 = 21$)

● How many candies are there exactly?

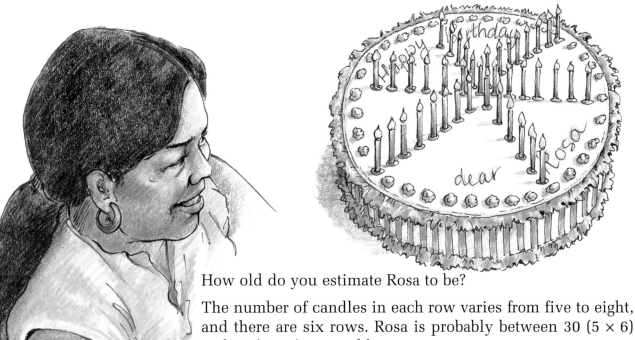

How old do you estimate Rosa to be?

The number of candles in each row varies from five to eight, and there are six rows. Rosa is probably between 30 (5 × 6) and 48 (8 × 6) years old.

You can improve on this estimate by taking a middle value of the number of candles in each row. In this case you can choose 6 or 7 or 6½. This gives Rosa's age as about thirty six (6 × 6), or forty two (7 × 6), or thirty nine (6½ × 6).

● **1.** What is Rosa's exact age according to the candles on her cake?

● **2.** Which value per row gives the best estimate?

In both these examples you got a reasonable estimate by splitting the whole amount into approximately equal parts. You split the candies into three approximately equal groups and the candles into six approximately equal groups. This enables you to multiply your estimate of the number in each group by the number of groups.

This method gives you a reasonable estimate **providing** that the groups are about equal and that your estimate of the number in each group is about right.

● **3.** Use this method to estimate the number in the stadium on pages 10 and 11. You have three numbers to multiply: the number of sections, the number of rows in a section, and the number of people in a row.

Use multiplication to calculate estimated answers to these problems. For one of them the method will not work. Which is the odd one out?

● About how many books do you estimate are in the bookcase?

14

● Tom has started to plant his flower bed for the Spring. Will he have enough plants to fill the bed?

José is opening a new store. He estimates that the average **wholesale** cost of a can of food is 60 cents. A shopkeeper usually has to buy in dozens, or sometimes in 6's or in 24's, from a wholesaler.

● How much do you estimate it will cost José to stock this wall of his store?

• About how many fish are in this tank?

• Guess the number of candies in the jar. There are approximately 40 candies in each layer.

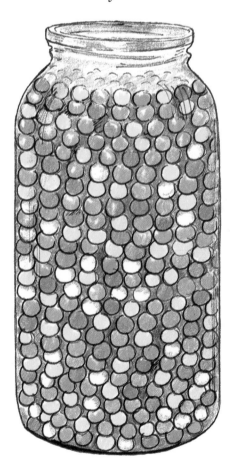

Estimating Large Numbers

Here are some estimates for you to try. A calculator will be useful. All the answers are large numbers.

● **1.** About how many hairs do you think there are on your head? One encyclopedia gives an estimate of 1 million; another says there are about 100,000. Which estimate do you think is best?

One way of finding out is to divide your head into equal sections, count the hairs in one section and then multiply the number of hairs in one section by the number of sections.

● **2.** About how long does it take to count to a million?

You could time yourself counting to 100, and then work out the number of 100's in a million, and multiply the two numbers.

● Do all numbers take the same time to say?

● **3.** About how many bricks do you think it takes to build a house?

☆ **Hint:**
It takes approximately 195 bricks to build a 10′ × 5′ wall.

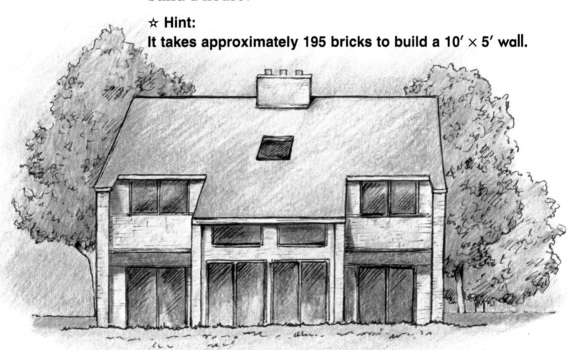

● **4.** What is your estimate for the number of leaves on a tree?

● **5.** Work out roughly how many words this book contains.

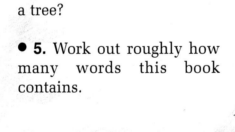

Approximate Cost

20 Sometimes it is useful to work out a rough, or estimated, answer to a problem. This estimate can be either a first step or a way of checking an answer you have tried to calculate exactly.

Ashley has $5 to spend on a quick meal. Can she afford a milk shake, French fries, and a cheeseburger?

Ashley does not need to figure out the bill exactly. She can just round each item up or down to the nearest dollar. If the price is less than 50 cents, round down to the nearest dollar. If the price is 50 cents or more, round up to the next dollar. Quickly total the dollars as an estimate of the cost.

● Andrew has $6.00 and wants a cheese pizza slice, fries, an ice cream, and a cola. Can he afford it? Just count to the nearest dollar for each item.

Number pairs

Andrew can get a more accurate estimate of the cost of his meal by thinking more carefully about how near to a dollar each amount is. One way is to pair or group amounts of cents which make about a dollar. For example 48 cents and 57 cents are each around 50 cents. Together they make just over a dollar.

● **1.** Which of these pairs make less than a dollar:
(a) 29 cents and 60 cents
(b) 29 cents and 72 cents
(c) 29 cents and 15 cents
(d) 29 cents and 30 cents

● **2.** Ted has paired these amounts to make about a dollar. He has taken one from each group each time. Is he correct?

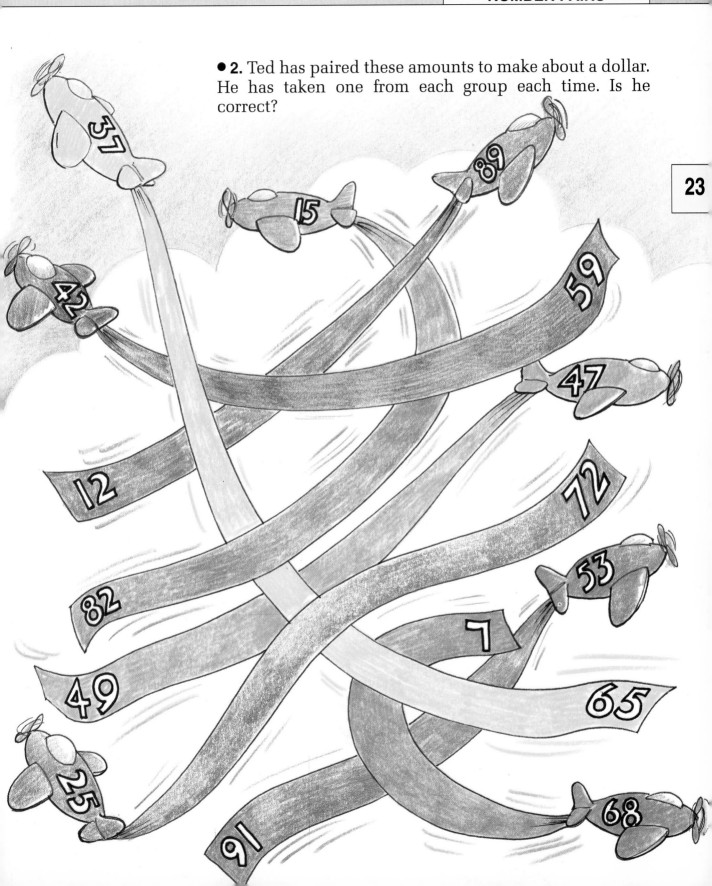

● Sam and Charlie have each estimated these bills to the near-est dollar. Who is the best at estimating?

Does My Answer Make Sense?

26

It is easy to make silly mistakes when figuring out a problem, especially when you press the wrong key on a calculator or write out a number incorrectly. It is a good idea to get into the habit of doing a quick estimate to check your answer.

You can learn several skills to help you do this.

Thinking about the number of digits

When you are calculating with figures, you can think about how many digits there should be in the answer.

If you have a problem like 494 + 721, you are adding hundreds, tens, and units to hundreds, tens, and units. You know that your answer must have at least have hundreds, tens, and units (three digits).

```
        H    T    U
        4    9    4+
        7    2    1
       _____
        ❏    ❏    ❏
```

But if you look at the left-hand side digits (the hundreds) of each figure, you can see that 4 + 7 = 11.
 Your answer will have four digits and be in the thousands.

```
     Th   H    T    U
         ④    9    4+
         ⑦    2    1
        _____
     ①   ❏    ❏    ❏
```

● **1.** Evelyn collects stamps. She has 852 in her U.S. album and 750 in her World album.

Does she have **(a)** Fewer than a thousand **(b)** more than a thousand? Do not add all the numbers, just the two you need.

● **2.** Ralph has seen a T-shirt for $10.50 that he wants to buy. He saves nickels and dimes. He counts up and finds he has 53 nickels and 55 dimes. Without calculating exactly, estimate whether or not Ralph has enough for the T-shirt.

The pupils of Oakville High School are collecting super-market stamps for new computer equipment. They need ten thousand stamps for the models they want to choose. The monthly totals for stamps collected are:

● Have they collected enough stamps?

☆ **Hint: you need to look at the two left-hand columns this time.**

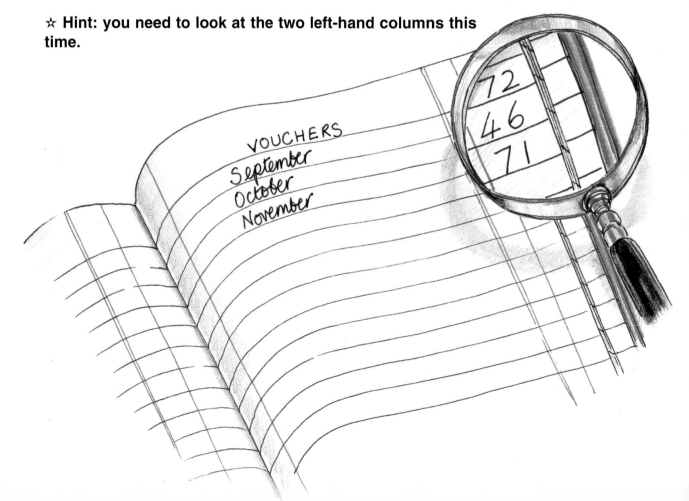

Grouping Similar Numbers Together

Carly's class sold raffle tickets to raise funds for Mother Theresa's work in Calcutta, India. Carly was responsible for collecting in the money. She kept a record in her notebook of how much each student raised.

1. We can group the numbers to make a quick estimate.

2. Shaquille, Lynette, Beverly, Dean, Jason and Neil have each raised about $25. There are six of them so that is about $150.

3. Jodie, Adam and Ethan each raised about $15, so that is another $45. The total must be about $195.

Sponsor amounts	
Shaquille	$ 25.12
Jodie	$ 15.78
Adam	$ 14.98
Lynette	$ 24.97
Beverly	$ 25.43
Dean	$ 24.05
Ethan	$ 15.04
Jason	$ 25.93
Neil	$ 24.78

Carly's teacher asks her how much she has collected so far. Carly adds the amount on her calculator and gets the total $181.10. Her teacher looks at the list and says that she does not think Carly's answer can be correct.

• What do you think Carly did wrong?

- Estimate the daily earnings of Cutcost supermarket.

Do not add up all the amounts. Take an easy number between the highest and lowest amounts and use that as a basis for your estimate.

CANNED FOODS

FROZEN MEAT
AND
MEAT PRODUCTS

30

09.03.9

NUMBER OF CHECKOUT	AMOUNT TO NEAREST DOLLAR
1	987
2	1007
3	1108
4	959
5	1297
6	1063
7	1154
8	930
9	879
10	937

• The Rocky Valley Recreation Center needs 100,000 customers per year to stay in business. These are the attendance figures for 10 days in March.

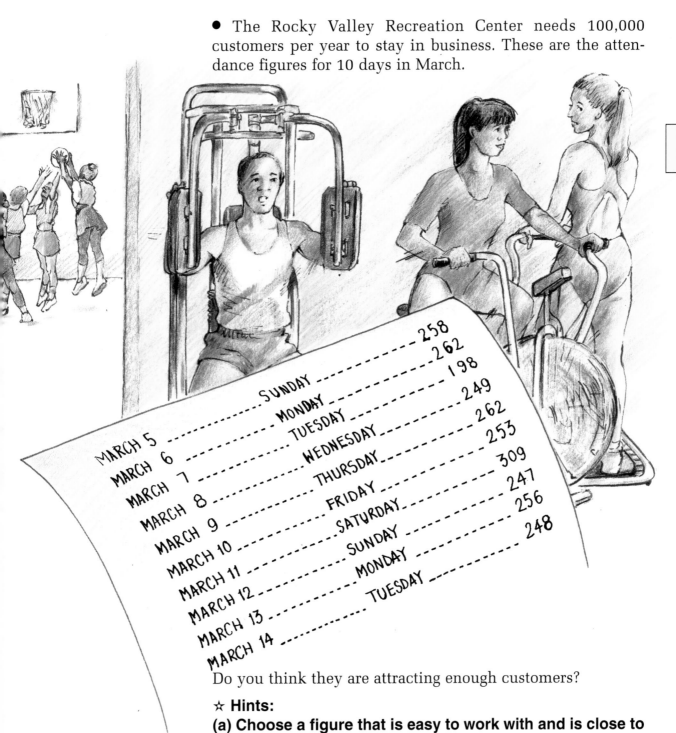

MARCH 5	SUNDAY	258
MARCH 6	MONDAY	262
MARCH 7	TUESDAY	198
MARCH 8	WEDNESDAY	249
MARCH 9	THURSDAY	262
MARCH 10	FRIDAY	253
MARCH 11	SATURDAY	309
MARCH 12	SUNDAY	247
MARCH 13	MONDAY	256
MARCH 14	TUESDAY	248

Do you think they are attracting enough customers?

☆ **Hints:**
(a) Choose a figure that is easy to work with and is close to most of the attendance figures.
(b) There are 365 days in a year.

Thinking About Whole Numbers

32

When you are dealing with decimals and fractions, concentrate on the whole numbers to make an estimate. It is similar to thinking about the dollars first when you get a bill.

Carrie is conducting an experiment about salt crystals. She has timed in seconds how long 3 different quantities of salt crystal take to dissolve in water.

These are her results:
170.2 seconds
5.43 seconds
7 seconds

She next needs to add the three results. What is the approximate total in seconds?

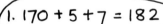
1. 170 + 5 + 7 = 182

2. Then there are .02 and .43

3. The answer will be between 182 and 183.

Carrie did not think about making an estimate. She wrote in her notebook:

$$
\begin{array}{r}
170.2 \\
5.43 \\
7 \\
\hline
175.70
\end{array}
$$

and got the answer 175.70

● **1.** What did she do wrong?

● Steve has handed in his homework without checking and thinking about the answers. Figure the answers to the nearest whole number to see which ones Steve has probably gotten wrong.

Do not do the whole problem.

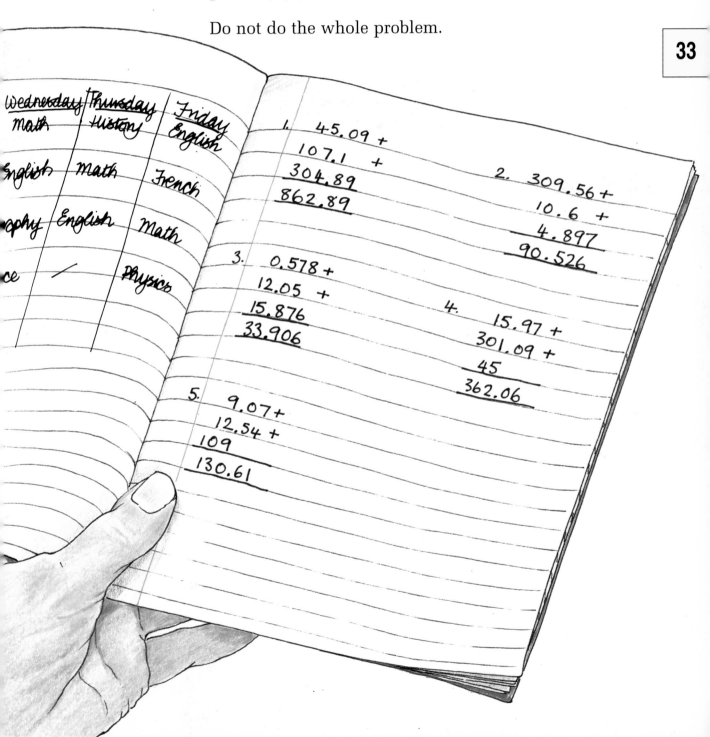

Wednesday | Thursday | Friday
math | History | English
English | math | French
ography | English | Math
ce | / | Physics

1. 45.09 +
107.1 +
304.89
862.89

2. 309.56 +
10.6 +
4.897
90.526

3. 0.578 +
12.05 +
15.876
33.906

4. 15.97 +
301.09 +
45
362.06

5. 9.07 +
12.54 +
109
130.61

Ken's mom has left him a list of chores she wants him to do before he goes to the baseball game in four hours.

34

Ken thinks there is too much to do and he will be late to the game.

● **1.** Is he right?
(Count the whole numbers and pair or group the fractions to make wholes.)

LeeAnn wants to pass her piano examination. Her teacher has told her she needs to practice ten hours a week. This is LeeAnn's diary for the week.

● **2.** Has LeeAnn done enough practicing this week?
(Count the whole numbers first and then pair off the fractions to make as them near as possible to a whole number.)

Chrissie is estimating how long it will take to cook the turkey for Thanksgiving. The recipe tells her to allow 20 minutes per pound, plus an extra 20 minutes. The bird weighs 16 lbs. 9 oz.

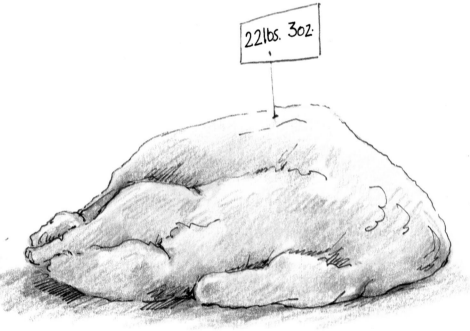

● How long will Jim's turkey take to cook?

Harry is estimating how much to charge for mowing the lawn. He wants to earn about $5 per hour.

This is a plan of the lawn. The lawn mower cuts a strip 20 inches wide.

36

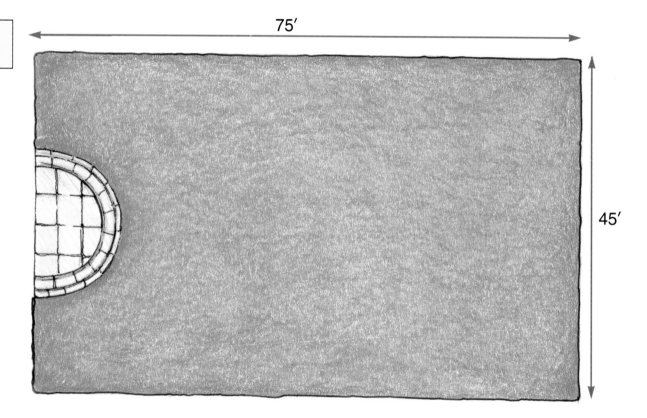

75′

45′

● How much do you think Harry should say he will charge?

☆ **Hints**
20 inches is just over 1½ feet.
Two strips will be about three feet.

Think about how long it will take Harry to mow one strip 75 feet long.

Allow time for getting the mower out, starting it up, turning the mower at the ends of each strip, and cleaning and putting away the mower at the end.

Multiplying by Powers of 10

When you multiply a number by 10, it has the effect of moving each digit to the left. The units become tens, the tens become hundreds, and so on. You have to put a zero in the units column to show that there are no units.

This makes it seem as if you just add a zero on the end of a number to multiply it by 10 because you do not see the numbers move.

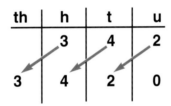

$\times 10$

Move each digit one place to right.

When you multiply by 100, it looks as if you add 2 zeros.

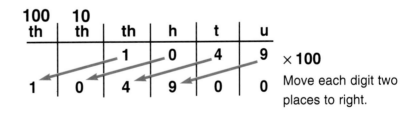

$\times 100$

Move each digit two places to right.

All the powers of 10 work the same way. The number of zeros in the power of 10, for example 3 zeros in 1,000, tells you how many places to the left the multiplied number moves and how many zeros to put on the end of it.

● How many zeros appear on the end of a number when you multiply it by a million?

Zero Bingo

A game for two players

You need two dice numbered 1 to 6, about 10 counters (or buttons or squares of paper), and a calculator.

Use the cards printed here.

400		180000			900		
2400	5000				300000		
	3000		12000			300	
150000	4000				2000		

200000			100	1200			
	10000		400		25000		
	80000	3600				1500	
6000				1600			2000

The rules

1. Each player must choose a card.

2. Decide who goes first.

3. Throw both dice. Multiply the number on each die by either 10 or 100. Multiply the new numbers together. If the product is one of the numbers on your card, cover that number with a counter.

4. The winner is the first player to get a covered line of numbers .

5. Use the calculator to check the products if there is any dispute about whether or not they are correct.

You can use what you know about multiplying by **powers** of 10 to estimate. It gives you a quick method of checking multiplications when any of the numbers in the problem are nearly 10, 100, 1,000, and so on.

Suppose you want to estimate how many tentacles 152 octopuses have.

152 × 8 is about the same as 150 × 10 so the answer must be about 1500. You need 4 digits in the answer.

Mr. Lee wants to buy an ornament for each of his 1,985 pupils to decorate the community Christmas tree. The ornaments cost 27 cents each. About how much will it cost in cents to buy one for each pupil?

● How much is this in dollars?

Challenge

● **1.** What is the largest product that can be made using the digits 1, 2, 3, 4, and 5?

What you know about multiplying by powers of 10 gives you a clue how to group the digits. You need a calculator to check your estimates.

Shed some light on the problem

● **2.** Mick the Miser saves the ends of his candles and melts them down to make new ones. From the ends of 10 candles he makes 1 new one. If he starts with 100 candles, how many can he burn?

Marco has decided to save up to buy a new bicycle. He earns $12 a week washing cars for his neighbors. He figures it will take him about a year to save up for the bicycle. His dad says it will take about six months.

● Who is better at estimating?

★ **Hint**
There are 52 weeks in a year.

About What Length?

Which of these two lines is longer?

44

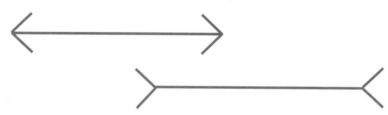

This is a well-known optical illusion, and you probably realized that the lines are in fact the same length.

When people first measured objects, they used parts of the body to help them. Two of the earliest units of length were the cubit and the span.

The disadvantage of using parts of the body for accurate measurement is that we come in all shapes and sizes.

Standardized lengths were introduced to overcome this problem. The one-foot ruler you use today was developed from the old way of measuring in feet.

Try measuring your foot against a 12"ruler.

Although parts of the body cannot give you accurate measurements, they are still useful for estimating.

Use a measuring tape to check whether these estimates work for you.

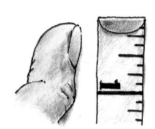

46

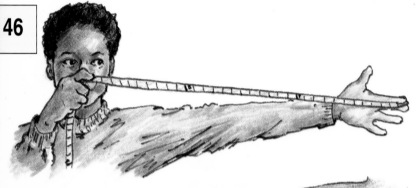

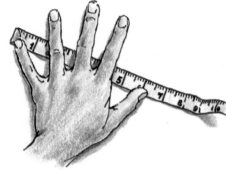

Draw a line 6 inches long. Ask some friends and adults to check their hand spans against the line.

● **1.** What body measurements can you use to help you estimate **(a)** the width of this book, **(b)** the length of your bathroom, **(c)** the diameter of your pencil, **(d)** the length of your bicycle, if you have one, **(e)** a yard of ribbon, **(f)** the width of a table.

Write down your estimates for **(a)** to **(f)**.

Check your answers by measuring.

● **2.** Which of these lines is about 3 inches long?

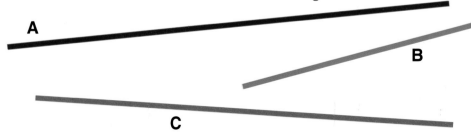

A

B

C

Estimate the lengths of these drawings to the nearest inch.
Check your estimates with a ruler.

You can make a party game of this. Assemble an interesting
collection of objects on a tray. Ask people to write down their
estimates of the length of each object to the nearest inch. You
can have larger things than are possible to draw in this book.

Have a competition with your friends. Choose a target length,
for example 11 inches. Each of you draw a line that you think
is the target length. Check with a ruler to see whose line is
nearest to the target length.

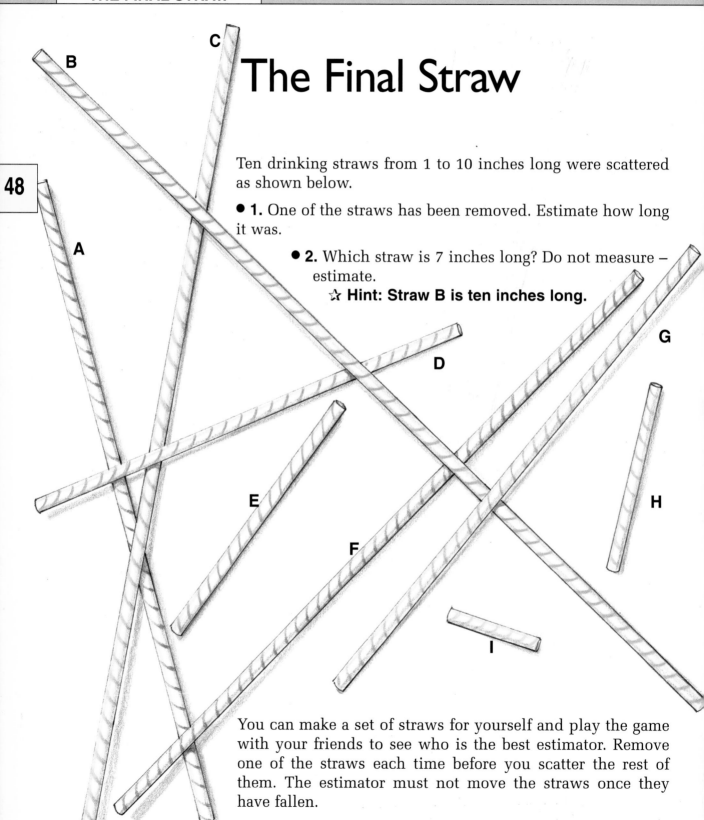

48

The Final Straw

Ten drinking straws from 1 to 10 inches long were scattered as shown below.

● **1.** One of the straws has been removed. Estimate how long it was.

● **2.** Which straw is 7 inches long? Do not measure – estimate.

☆ **Hint: Straw B is ten inches long.**

You can make a set of straws for yourself and play the game with your friends to see who is the best estimator. Remove one of the straws each time before you scatter the rest of them. The estimator must not move the straws once they have fallen.

About How Tall?

Sometimes it is useful to be able to estimate a height.

One way of finding a good estimate of a height is to compare the estimated object with a height you already know. Because most adult men are about 6 feet tall, this is one of the easiest heights to use in estimating. This is only a rough guide but is often helpful.

● Estimate the heights of **(a)** a door, **(b)** a room, **(c)** a two story house, **(d)** a single-decker bus, **(e)** [te]the seat of a chair from the floor, **(f)** a cat.

Stepping Off

50

If you know, or can estimate fairly accurately, the length or height of one object, you can use it to estimate the length or height of others.

● The height of an adult man is usually about 6 feet. How long do you estimate this car to be?

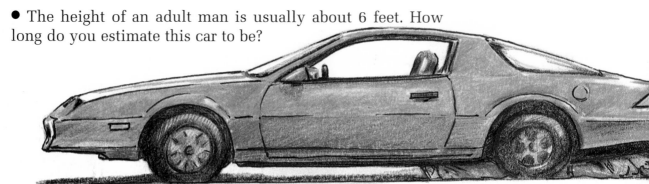

You can estimate the length of the car just by looking at the length of the mechanic and comparing the two lengths by eye. If you want a more accurate estimate from a drawing, you can mark off on a piece of paper the length of the mechanic and use the paper as a scale to step off along the car.

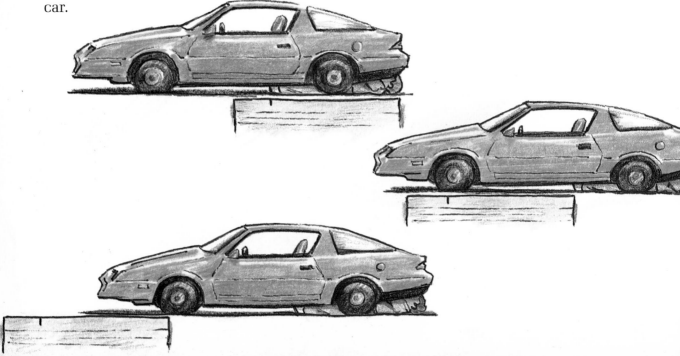

Make your own scale on paper and use it to step off for these estimates.

● **1.** About how tall are these trees?

You can use the scale the other way around as well.

● **2.** About what fraction of the man is the tree?

● **3.** About how tall is the apple tree?

● **1.** About how wide is this tree?

● **2.** About how long is this pine cone?

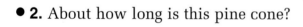

● **3.** About how long is this bridge?

● The rowboat is about 10 feet long. About how long are the whales?

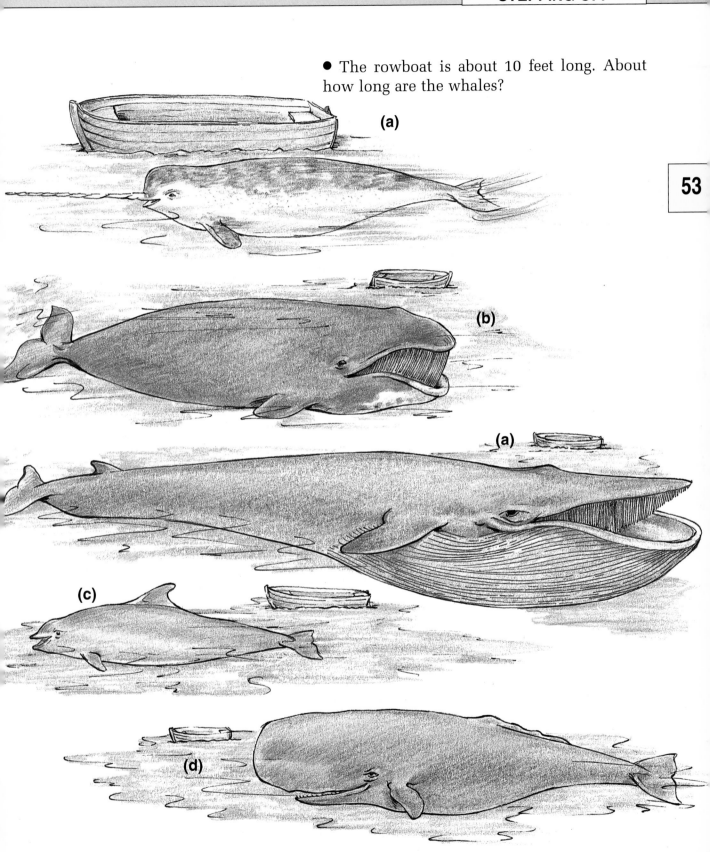

(a)

(b)

(a)

(c)

(d)

● **1.** About how tall was Tyrannosaurus Rex?

● **2.** Estimate the length of its teeth.

● **3.** Estimate the wing-span of this pterodactyl.

Perspective

The idea of stepping off one object against another in a drawing works only if they are both drawn to the same scale. You cannot use the man in this picture to estimate the height of the church tower because the artist has used **perspective** to give an illusion of distance.

In reality, too, it is more difficult to estimate the height of a distant tree than one you can stand by. The further away an object is, the smaller it looks.

When we know the actual height of something in the distance, the size it appears to be helps us to estimate how far away it is.

When you have to estimate both the distance and the height of an unfamiliar object, it is very difficult unless you can also see something you already know the height and distance of.

Try to get into the habit of looking carefully at the things around you and estimating their **dimensions**. When you travel by car, look at the mileage on the road signs to develop your skill in estimating long distances. Estimate the speed at which you are traveling and then check on the speedometer to see how good or bad your guess was.

How Much Does It Hold?

It can be quite difficult to estimate how much a bottle or pitcher holds. These containers each hold the same amount of liquid.

Investigation

You need a pint measuring cup.

Collect as many differently shaped pitchers, bottles, glasses, and cartons as you can. Try to find ones that do not have the capacity marked on them. For each container, first estimate whether they hold more or less than a pint. Write down your estimates.

1. Fill a pint measuring cup with water. Now pour the water into each container in turn and see how good your estimates were. If the container holds a pint or more, mark a pint line on it. One way to mark the container is to use masking tape.

2. Mark where you estimate the half pint ,line to be on each container. Fill the measuring cup with ½ pint of water. Pour the water into each container to see how accurate you were this time.

● **3.** Is the half-pint mark always halfway down the side from the pint mark?

More or Less Than a Half?

1. Are these containers more or less than half full?

Remember that for some containers, half full is not the same as halfway down the side.

1.

2.

3.

4.

5.

6.

7.

About How Much Is Left?

58

If you know the total capacity of a container that is only part full, you can use your judgment of half and quarter full to estimate the amount that is remaining.

Estimate these quantities. Use halfs and quarters of the total capacity to help you.

- **1.** About how many ounces are left?
- **2.** About how many ounces are left?
- **3.** About how many glasses full are left?
- **4.** How many pints are left?
- **5.** About how many pounds of potatoes are left in the bag?
- **6.** About how many gallons are left?

> 1 gallon = 4 quarts
> 1 quart = 2 pints
> 1 pint = 2 cups
> 1 cup = 8 ounces
>
> 1LB = 16 ounces

1.

2.

3.

4.

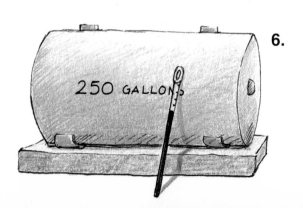

5.

6.

Glossary

capacity the amount a container can hold

cubit an ancient unit of measurement of length, which was approximately the length of an adult's forearm from elbow to finger tip

diameter the distance across a circle passing through its center

digit a numeral from 0 to 9

dimensions an amount that can be measured such as length, width, height, area, or volume

estimate an approximate judgment of size, time, cost, or any other measurement

optical illusion something that deceives our eyes

perspective the art of drawing to give the appearance of distance

power the number of times a number is multiplied by itself. For example 2 to the power 3 (2^3) is $2 \times 2 \times 2 = 8$.

span the distance between the thumb and little finger when the fingers are stretched apart

wholesale store owners buy goods at a cheaper price from suppliers because they buy larger quantities than an ordinary customer

wing-span the distance between wing tips when wings are spread

Answers

Page 6 and 7
It takes about 15 minutes to walk a mile. The eye of a needle is about 1/30 of an inch.

Pages 8 and 9
All the statements except 6, 8 and 9 are estimates or approximations.

Pages 10 and 11
1. Some people might be let in through a gate or door, or climb through or over the fence. Some people who bought tickets beforehand might not have come that day.
2. See pages 12 and 13.

Page 12
There are exactly twenty two candies.

Page 13
1. Rosa has forty one candles on her cake.
2. The value 6½ for the number of candles in a row gives the best estimate of Rosa's age.
3. There are 8 segments in the stadium, each with about 12 rows. The number of people in each row varies from about 12 to 16. Take a middle value of 14 for the number in a row. There are about $8 \times 12 \times 14 = 1,344$ people – or between 1,300 and 1,400.

Page 14
There are about 15 books on each shelf, and 5 shelves. $15 \times 5 = 75$. There are about 75 books all together.

Page 15
The two middle rows of each segment have 6 and 7 plants, so take 7 as the average number needed for a row. There are 4 rows in each segment and 3 more segments to plant. That will take about $7 \times 4 \times 3 = 84$ plants. Then Tom needs about 5 more plants for the inner circle. That gives a total of about 89 plants needed. Tom has 3 full boxes with about 6 rows, with 4 plants in each row. That is $3 \times 6 \times 4 = 72$ plants. He also has 12 plants left in a box. All together he has about 84 plants, so he probably won't have enough. He will have to plant the rest a little further apart.

Page 16
There are 6 shelves with approximately 12 cans on each shelf. Pablo will need approximately $6 \times 12 = 72$ cans to fill the shelves. He will need to buy about a dozen of each at 60 cents each, which will cost about 60 cents $\times 12 \times 72 = \$518.40$. He should allow between \$500 and \$550.

Page 17
The fish are not spread evenly through the tank so you cannot use multiplication to make an estimate. This is the odd one out.

There are about 40 candies in each layer and about 25 layers. A reasonable estimate is $60 \times 25 = 1,000$ candies all together.

Pages 18 and 19
1. This example shows the difficulty of estimating very large numbers. The thickness and number of hairs on people's heads varies considerably.
2. It takes about 1 minute to count to 100. At this rate, it takes approximately 10,000 minutes, which is nearly 7 days, to count to a million. The larger numbers

will take longer to say, so about 10 days is a reasonable estimate. Could you stay awake that long?

3. It takes about 12,000 bricks to build a four bedroom detached house.

4. This depends on the size of the tree. One way is to count the leaves on part of a branch and then multiply. Another method is to wait until the Fall, mark out a square foot on the ground, count the leaves in it, and multiply the number of square feet of ground covered by the approximate number of leaves in each one.

5. About 7,500. The best way is to count the number of words in each of three or four lines to get a reasonable estimate of the number of words per line. Then find an estimate for the number of lines on a page in a similar way, by looking at three or four pages. Then calculate from the page numbers how many pages are actually filled with text. Finally, multiply the three numbers.

Page 21
Andrew can afford the meal he wants. It comes to 5 whole dollars, and the extra cents are less than a dollar.

Page 22 and 23
1. Each pair except **(b)** equals less than a dollar.
2. Ted is correct except for 7 and 68, which make less than a dollar, and 91 and 53, which make more than a dollar.

Pages 24 and 25
The actual totals are:
1. $7.11 **2.** $17.05
3. $94.66 **4.** $106.07
Sam is better at estimating than Charlie

because Charlie does not group pairs or threes of cents to the nearest dollar.

Page 27
1. 8 and **7** make 15. There is an extra digit in the answer so **(b)** Evelyn has more than one thousand stamps

2. Ralph has less than $10.50. 55 dimes is $5.50; a nickel is worth half a dime, so 53 nickels cannot be the other $5 Ralph needs.

Page 28
Yes, they have collected enough. If you look at the left hand side numbers, $3 \times 3 = 9$, which is not quite enough. But the numbers in the *next* column total over 10 so there will be 1 to carry. 9 + the 1 that is carried = 10, which makes an extra digit, and the answer will have a number in the 10,000 column.

Page 29
Carly missed one of the students who collected about $15.

Page 30
The daily earnings are about $10 \times \$1,000 = \$10,000$

Page 31
If you take 250 as representing a day's attendance, there will be about 250×365 customers per year.
$250 \times 4 \times 100 = 100,000$. 365 is less than 400 ($4 \times 100$), so the recreation center is probably going to be in trouble.

Page 32
1. Carrie forgot to write 7 as 7.00. She counted 7 as 0.07

Page 33
Steve has been very careless in writing out the problems and did not keep the

decimal points in line. The only answers that can possibly be correct are **4.** and **5.**

Page 34

1. Ken has plenty of time to do the chores. They should take less than 3 hours.
2. LeeAnn has done 8 whole hours and 2½ hours in fractions of an hour. She has reached her target.

Page 35

Jim's turkey will take over 7 hours (22 ÷ 3) plus 20 minutes. He should allow nearly eight hours.

Page 36

Harry will need to walk about 30 strips (45 ÷ 3 × 2). Allow 3 minutes per strip. That is 90 minutes. Allow about 15 minutes for getting ready and putting away. Harry should charge about $9.

Page 37

6 zeros

Page 41

$540

Page 42

1. 431 × 52 = 22,412
2. From 100 ends he makes 10 candles. From those 10 ends he makes 1 candle. He burns 111 candles all together.

Page 43

There are 52 weeks in year. $12 × 52 will be a bit more than $10 × 50, which is $500. In six months, Marco will earn half as much – about $250. Marco's dad's esti-mate sounds about right.

Page 46

1. (a) thumb **(b)** a pace or a cubit or a span **(c)** thumb **(d)** pace **(e)** nose to finger tip **(f)** span

2. (b)

Page 48

1. 4 inches
2. A

Page 49

(a), **(e)**, and **(f)** check by measuring; **(b)** usually about 8 feet, although some old houses have rooms about 6 feet tall, and some large rooms have high ceilings; **(c)** about 22 feet for a modern house – it depends on the pitch of the roof; old houses are sometimes not so tall; **(d)** about 8 feet.

Page 50

The car is about 15 feet long

Page 51

1. (a) about 9 feet **(b)** about 30 feet **(c)** about 360 feet
2. about ⅓ **3.** about 2 feet

Page 52

1. about 25 feet **2.** about 26 inches
3. about 180 feet

Page 53

(a) about 14 feet **(b)** about 60 feet **(c)** about 95 feet **(d)** about 30 feet **(e)** about 80 feet

Page 54

1. about 33 feet
2. about 4 inches **3.** about 25 feet

Page 56

3. No

Page 57

3. 4. 5. and **6.** are less than half. The rest are more than half.

Page 58

1. about 4 oz. **2.** about 6 oz.
3. about 1 glass full **4.** about 6 pints
5. about 11 lbs. **6.** about 190 gallons

Index